COLUMBUS DAY

RENNAY CRAATS

www.av2books.com

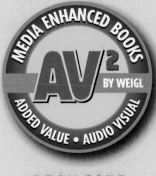

MEDIA ENHANCED BOOKS
AV²
BY WEIGL
ADDED VALUE • AUDIO VISUAL

BOOK CODE

W 5 1 5 3 7 8

AV² by Weigl brings you media enhanced books that support active learning.

AV² provides enriched content that supplements and complements this book. Weigl's AV² books strive to create inspired learning and engage young minds for a total learning experience.

Go to **www.av2books.com**, and enter this book's unique code. You will have access to video, audio, web links, quizzes, a slide show, and activities.

Audio
Listen to sections of the book read aloud.

Video
Watch informative video clips.

Web Link
Find research sites and play interactive games.

Try This!
Complete activities and hands-on experiments.

Due to the dynamic nature of the Internet, some of the URLs and activities provided as part of AV² by Weigl may have changed or ceased to exist. AV² by Weigl accepts no responsibility for any such changes. All media enhanced books are regularly monitored to update addresses and sites in a timely manner. Contact AV² by Weigl at 1-866-649-3445 or av2books@weigl.com with any questions, comments, or feedback.

Published by AV² by Weigl
350 5ᵗʰ Avenue, 59ᵗʰ Floor
New York, NY 10118
Web site: www.av2books.com   www.weigl.com

Library of Congress Cataloging-in-Publication Data

Craats, Rennay.
 Columbus Day / Rennay Craats.
   p. cm. -- (American celebrations)
 Originally published: 2004.
 Includes index.
 ISBN 978-1-60596-775-2 (hardcover : alk. paper) -- ISBN 978-1-60596-933-6 (softcover : alk. paper) --
 ISBN 978-1-60596-940-4 (e-book)
 1. Columbus Day--Juvenile literature. 2. Columbus, Christopher--Juvenile literature. 3. America--Discovery and exploration--Spanish--Juvenile literature. I. Title.
 E120.C88 2011
 394.264--dc22
                           2009050986

Printed in the United States of America in North Mankato, Minnesota
1 2 3 4 5 6 7 8 9 0 14 13 12 11 10

052010
WEP264000

Editor Heather C. Hudak   **Design** Terry Paulhus

Weigl acknowledges Getty Images as its primary image supplier for this book.

Every reasonable effort has been made to trace ownership and to obtain permission to reprint copyright material. The publishers would be pleased to have any errors or omissions brought to their attention so that they may be corrected in subsequent printings.

CONTENTS

What is Columbus Day?

On the second Monday of October, American families celebrate Columbus Day. This holiday celebrates the day that Christopher Columbus became the first European to discover the Americas. Columbus and his crew landed on San Salvador, Central America, on October 12, 1492.

⭐ Christopher Columbus never explored the land that became the United States of America. He landed on the island of Puerto Rico.

Christopher Columbus was courageous. While most people believed Earth was flat, Columbus believed Earth was round. It was thought that ships would fall off the "edge of the world." Columbus disagreed and sailed west in search of Asia. Later, Columbus found land. He thought he had discovered a new route to Asia. Instead, he found the Americas. When Columbus died in 1506, he did not know that he had discovered the Americas.

Special Events
THROUGHOUT THE YEAR

JANUARY 1
NEW YEAR'S DAY

FEBRUARY (THIRD MONDAY)
PRESIDENTS' DAY

MARCH 17
ST. PATRICK'S DAY

SUNDAY IN MARCH OR APRIL
EASTER

MAY (LAST MONDAY)
MEMORIAL DAY

JUNE 14
FLAG DAY

JULY 4
INDEPENDENCE DAY

AUGUST (FIRST SUNDAY)
FAMILY DAY

SEPTEMBER (FIRST MONDAY)
LABOR DAY

OCTOBER (SECOND MONDAY)
COLUMBUS DAY

NOVEMBER 11
VETERANS DAY

DECEMBER 25
CHRISTMAS DAY

Columbus Day History

During the late 1400s, **navigators** and scientists began to claim that the world was round and not flat. Some navigators insisted that the Atlantic Ocean was only a small body of water, and that the distance between Spain and India could be covered by a boat in a few days.

Christopher Columbus, an Italian navigator, was asked by the king and queen of Spain to find a shorter route west across the Atlantic Ocean. In 1492, Columbus and his crew set off with three ships.

✰ Columbus and his crew set foot on land on October 12, 1492, after 36 days of sailing.

Navigators in the 1400s and 1500s used tools, such as calipers for measuring distance, and telescopes for surveying the land.

Later, he landed on an island in the Caribbean. Columbus thought he had found the East Indies.

Until his death in 1506, Columbus believed he had reached Asia. Although he was mistaken, his explorations of the Americas helped Spain become the richest nation in Europe. Portuguese sailors followed the Spanish ships across the Atlantic Ocean, and soon, they also traded in the Americas. Columbus is celebrated because, without him, the United States might not exist. His expedition led to the first permanent **colonies** in the New World.

Past and Present Celebrations

ITALIAN-AMERICANS first observed the anniversary of Columbus's arrival in the New World in 1792. It was a 300th anniversary celebration hosted by the Columbian Order of New York.

THE FIRST official celebration of Christopher Columbus by the government was in 1892. President Benjamin Harrison urged the people of the United States to celebrate the 400th anniversary of Columbus's landing in the New World. It was not called Columbus Day.

COLUMBUS DAY officially became a national holiday in the United States in 1937. The day was filled with parades and other ceremonies and festivities. Columbus Day is still celebrated in much the same way today. The day is celebrated as an important part of United States' history.

Important People

Christopher Columbus was born in Genoa, Italy, in 1451. When Columbus was young, he worked with his mother and father as a wool weaver. Columbus began a seafaring career when he was 14 years old. At the time, Europeans sailed around Africa to reach Asia. Columbus believed that a faster route to Asia could be found by sailing west.

For years, Columbus asked the leaders of European countries to pay for his trip. In return, he promised to find a faster route to Asia. No one was willing to pay for his trip. In 1492, Columbus talked to King Ferdinand V and Queen Isabella I of Spain. They gave him money for his voyage.

⭐Christopher Columbus studied for many hours to become a captain. To learn all he could about the world, he studied The Bible, map making, geography, and the writings of other explorers.

On August 3, 1492, three ships and 90 sailors set sail from Spain. The ships were called the *Nina*, the *Pinta*, and the *Santa Maria*.

✦✦ **Christopher Columbus formed a colony near Cape Isabella, in the Dominican Republic. This was the first European settlement in the New World.**

When Christopher Columbus and his crew finally reached land, they believed they were in Asia. They dressed in their best clothes to meet the local leaders. The people they met were not Asian. They were the **indigenous peoples** of South America. The sailors had landed in the Bahamas, on an island named Guanahani. Columbus renamed the area San Salvador. He claimed it for Spain.

First-hand Account

"The land was first seen by a sailor called Rodrigo de Triana, although the Admiral at ten o'clock that evening standing on the quarter-deck saw a light, but so small a body that he could not affirm it to be land;…At two o'clock in the morning the land was discovered, at two **leagues**' distance; They took in sail and remained under the square-sail lying to till day, which was Friday, when they found themselves near a small island, one of the Lucayos, called in the Indian language Guanahani."

Christopher Columbus

Columbus Day Celebrations

Christopher Columbus's discovery was not celebrated in the United States for 300 years. In 1792, New York held a ceremony to honor Columbus. Soon after, the city of Washington was named the District of Columbia in honor of Columbus's discovery. People of Italian heritage living in New York City wanted to officially honor Columbus. They were very proud of him.

⭐⭐ Columbus's arrival in the New World was important to many countries. As a result, Columbus Day celebrations are held in many parts of the world.

In 1866, they organized events to celebrate Columbus and his discovery of the Americas. The next year, more Italian organizations across the country held celebrations, too. People of Italian heritage in San Francisco were the first to name their celebration Columbus Day.

Since 1971, the national holiday has been celebrated on the second Monday in October. During this long weekend, families and friends across the U.S. gather to celebrate Columbus Day.

Discovery Around the World

CANADA

Discovery Day is celebrated in the province of Newfoundland and Labrador on the Monday nearest June 24. It celebrates the discovery of the province by John Cabot in 1497.

SPAIN

On October 12, Spain celebrates National Day. This holiday honors the Spanish monarchy that funded Columbus's voyages. A huge military parade is held in Madrid on this day.

ARGENTINA

Argentina and other Latin American countries celebrate Día de la Raza, or Day of the Race, on October 12. This holiday commemorates the combining of European and New World cultures.

Celebrating Today

Since Christopher Columbus was Italian, many Columbus Day celebrations involve people of Italian heritage. Many Columbus Day parades have an Italian theme. These celebrations often feature Italian-American celebrities and traditional dancing and music. Christopher Columbus, his culture, and traditions are honored. Today, many U.S. citizens celebrate the second Monday in October by enjoying the sights, sounds, and tastes of local Italian culture.

Some people celebrate Columbus Day at parades and festivals. Most major cities host parades or festivals during the holiday weekend. Some people have small neighborhood festivals and parades. Many spend the day relaxing with their friends and family.

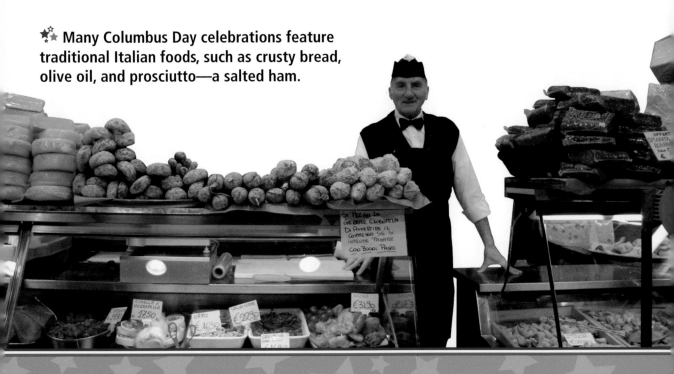

★★ Many Columbus Day celebrations feature traditional Italian foods, such as crusty bread, olive oil, and prosciutto—a salted ham.

Some people do not think Columbus Day should be celebrated. They do not believe that Columbus was a hero because the discovery of the Americas by Europeans led to the death of many American Indians.

Columbus Day in the United States

Columbus Day is celebrated across the United States. This map shows a few events that take place each year on the second Monday in October.

ILLINOIS Thousands of people attend the Columbus Day Parade in Chicago. The floats, bands, and local and state celebrities form a parade that is more than 1 mile long.

California

CALIFORNIA Every year, the biggest Columbus Day parade in the West takes place in San Francisco. The Italian Heritage Parade offers food, floats, and other activities, such as car shows.

Hawai'i

0	970 Miles

Alaska

0	1,278 Miles

NEW YORK New York City hosts the biggest Columbus Day celebration in the U.S. New York's large Italian- American community honors Christopher Columbus and the discovery of the Americas.

New York

New Jersey

Illinois

NEW JERSEY Each year, Ocean County, New Jersey, hosts a Columbus Day Parade and Italian Festival. The celebration honors Columbus's discovery. It also celebrates Italian heritage in the United States. The parade is filled with clowns, floats, and bands.

FLORIDA In Miami, people celebrate Columbus Day on the water. The annual Columbus Day **regatta** has drawn sailors since 1954. To honor Columbus, sailors compete in a race in Biscayne Bay.

Florida

N
W   E
S

0   207 Miles

Columbus Day Symbols

American citizens have honored Christopher Columbus in many ways. Several cities in states such as Georgia, Ohio, Nebraska, and Mississippi have been named after the navigator, and **monuments** across the United States honor Christopher Columbus, his voyages, and his discovery of the Americas.

COLUMBUS MEMORIAL FOUNTAIN

The Columbus Memorial Fountain is in Washington, D.C. It was erected in 1912 by the U.S. Congress and the Knights of Columbus to honor Columbus's spirit of discovery and his opening of the New World. The inscription reads, "To the memory of Christopher Columbus whose high faith and indomitable courage gave to mankind a new world. Born 1451—Died 1506."

ITALIAN FLAG

Many Italian-Americans observe Columbus Day as a celebration of their heritage. Columbus Day was first promoted by an Italian-American as a day to appreciate the contributions of Italian-Americans and celebrate Italian pride, much like St. Patrick's Day is a celebration of Irish pride.

SANTA MARIA

Columbus's ship, the *Santa Maria*, was the largest of the three ships Columbus used for his first trip across the Atlantic. The other ships were the *Nina* and the *Pinta*. Columbus himself was sailing on the *Santa Maria* when he landed in the Americas.

A Song to Remember

"In 1492 Columbus Sailed the Ocean Blue," is a song that is often heard on Columbus Day. It helps people remember the details of Columbus's journey. Here are the first eight **stanzas** of the song.

In fourteen hundred ninety-two
Columbus sailed the ocean blue.

He had three ships and left from Spain;
He sailed through sunshine, wind, and rain.

He sailed by night; he sailed by day;
He used the stars to find his way.

A compass also helped him know
How to find the way to go.

Ninety sailors were on board;
Some men worked while others snored.

Then the workers went to sleep;
And others watched the ocean deep.

Day after day they looked for land;
They dreamed of trees and rocks
and sand.

October 12 their dream
came true,
You never saw a happier crew!

- Unknown

Write Your Own Song

Songwriting is a fun way to express thoughts and ideas. Get creative, and write your own song.

Listen to a song that you like, and pay attention to the words. Which words rhyme? How many verses are there? How many lines are in each verse? How many times is the chorus sung?

Start brainstorming ideas. What do you want your song to be about? Choose an event, idea, person, or feeling you would like to write about.

Write the verses. Songs usually have three or four verses. Each one will be different but should relate to the chorus.

Think of a tune for your song. Some songwriters like to write the tune before the words. Others will write them at the same time.

Many songwriters work with other people to create songs. Try working with a classmate or friend to think of a tune or words for your song.

Write the chorus to your song. The chorus is the main idea of the song. It connects the verses together.

Making a Juice Box Sailboat

Making your own juice box sailboat is a great way to learn how sailboats work.

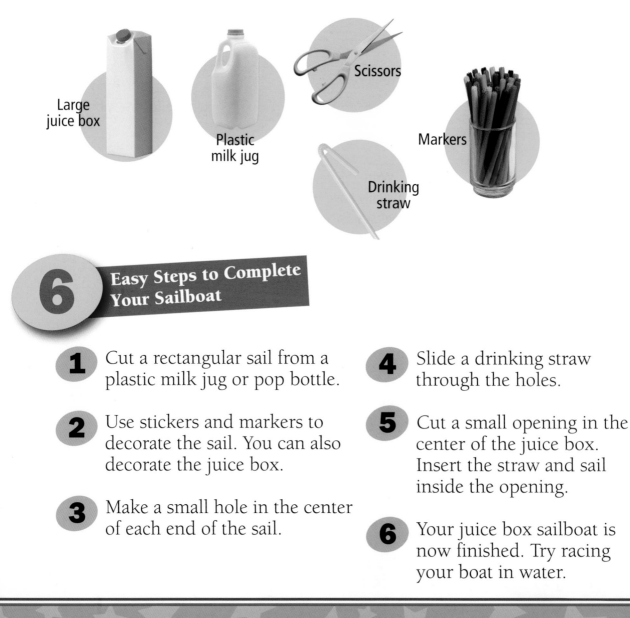

Large juice box

Plastic milk jug

Scissors

Drinking straw

Markers

6 Easy Steps to Complete Your Sailboat

1 Cut a rectangular sail from a plastic milk jug or pop bottle.

2 Use stickers and markers to decorate the sail. You can also decorate the juice box.

3 Make a small hole in the center of each end of the sail.

4 Slide a drinking straw through the holes.

5 Cut a small opening in the center of the juice box. Insert the straw and sail inside the opening.

6 Your juice box sailboat is now finished. Try racing your boat in water.

Make a Columbus Day Boat

Ingredients

18 marshmallows
9 maraschino cherries
vanilla ice cream
butterscotch syrup

Equipment

ice cream scoop
12 toothpicks
3 plates
spoon
can opener

paper
markers
scissors
tape

Directions

1. Place three scoops of ice cream on each plate. Spoon butterscotch syrup on top of each scoop.
2. Make nine sandwiches by placing a cherry between two marshmallows. Use a toothpick to hold your sandwich together.
3. Put one toothpick in each scoop of ice cream.
4. Cut a rectangular piece of paper, and tape it onto another toothpick. This will be your boat's flag. Use markers to decorate the flag.
5. Place the toothpick flag on top of the middle marshmallow on each plate. You have made ice cream copies of the *Nina*, the *Pinta*, and the *Santa Maria*.

Test Your Knowledge!

1
When did Christopher Columbus reach the Americas?

2
When did the first official Columbus Day celebration take place in the United States?

3
What are three symbols of Columbus Day?

4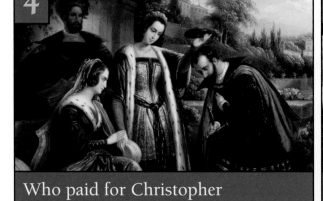
Who paid for Christopher Columbus's voyage to the Americas?

5
What are three foods eaten on Columbus Day?

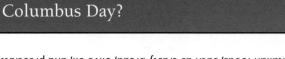

Quiz Answers:
1. Christopher Columbus first reached the Americas on October 12, 1492.
2. The first official Columbus Day celebration took place on October 12, 1892.
3. Three symbols of Columbus Day are the Columbus Memorial Fountain, the Italian flag, and the *Santa Maria*.
4. King Ferdinand V and Queen Isabella I paid for Columbus's voyage.
5. Italian foods, such as crusty bread, olive oil, and prosciutto, are eaten on Columbus Day.

Glossary

colonies: areas that are ruled by a more powerful country

indigenous peoples: the first people to inhabit a place

leagues: an old measure of distance equal to about 3 miles

monuments: large objects that are often made of stone and meant to honor someone or something

navigators: the people who direct ships

regatta: organized boat or yacht races

stanzas: groups of lines in a poem that have a fixed length, meter, or rhyme pattern and make up sections of the poem

Index

Log on to www.av2books.com

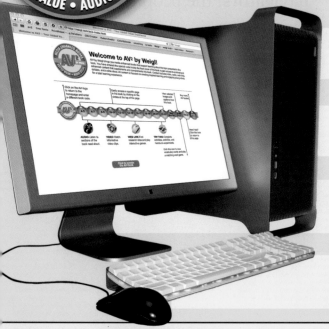

AV[2] by Weigl brings you media enhanced books that support active learning. Go to **www.av2books.com**, and enter the special code inside the front cover of this book. You will gain access to enriched and enhanced content that supplements and complements this book. Content includes video, audio, web links, quizzes, a slide show, and activities.

Audio
Listen to sections of the book read aloud.

Video
Watch informative video clips.

Web Link
Find research sites and play interactive games.

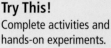

Try This!
Complete activities and hands-on experiments.

WHAT'S ONLINE?

Try This!
Complete activities and hands-on experiments.

Pages 8-9 Write a biography about an important person

Pages 10-11 Describe the features and special events of a similar celebration around the world

Pages 14-15 Complete a mapping activity about Columbus Day celebrations

Pages 16-17 Try this activity about important holiday symbols

Pages 20-21 Play an interactive activity

Web Link
Find research sites and play interactive games.

Pages 6-7 Find out more about the history of Columbus Day

Pages 10-11 Learn more about similar celebrations around the world

Pages 16-17 Find information about important holiday symbols

Pages 18-19 Link to more information about Columbus Day

Pages 20-21 Check out more holiday craft ideas

Video
Watch informative video clips.

Pages 4-5 Watch a video about Columbus Day

Pages 12-13 Check out a video about how people celebrate Columbus Day

EXTRA FEATURES

Audio
Hear introductory audio at the top of every page

Key Words
Study vocabulary, and play a matching word game.

Slide Show
View images and captions, and try a writing activity.

AV[2] Quiz
Take this quiz to test your knowledge